MONUMENTAL
SAGRADA FAMÍLIA

D1282233

MONUMENTAL
SAGRADA
FAMÍLIA

Catalunya Desapareguda series

First edition: March 2017

© Daniel Venteo i Meléndrez, texts and selection of images

© Pep Daudé/Basílica de la Sagrada Família, photographs

© Editorial Efadós, this edition

    Carrer d'Edison, 3 · Nau A
    Polígon industrial les Torrenteres
    08754 El Papiol (Baix Llobregat)
    Telèfon 93 673 12 12
    efados@efados.cat
    www.efados.cat

© Editorial Efadós, in the Catalunya Desapareguda series

Design and phototypesetting: Editorial Efadós

Language advice: M. Neus Doncel Saumell

Translation: Lexikos Traduccions

The author would like to thank José Manuel Almuzara, Francisco Arauz, Jordi Bonet i Armengol, Gabriel Carrió, Jordi Faulí, Íngrid Gómez, Jesús Serdio, Jaume Serrallonga, Josep Tallada and Laia Vinaixa

ISBN 978-84-16547-59-3
DL B 5886-2017
Printed in Catalonia

MONUMENTAL
SAGRADA
FAMÍLIA

PROLOGUE

JORDI FAULÍ

*Chief architect and coordinator of work
on the Sagrada Família*

When the scaffolding was removed from the first spire of the Nativity façade, named after Saint Barnabas, on 30th November 1925, a worker on the site exclaimed, "Fa goig" (a Catalan expression meaning literally that something makes you feel joyful), greatly pleasing the architect. Throughout the day he told everybody he met about this, comparing it to the "gaudium magnum" of the Three Kings when they saw the star. This "Fa goig" expressed that it felt good to look at its extraordinary beauty, that it touched the heart. Gaudí liked this: it was what he wanted for every part of the Sagrada Família. This beauty touches the heart of visitors to the church, wherever they come from.

Antoni Gaudí designed all the contents and meaning of the Sagrada Família as an expression of his profoundly-felt Christian faith. He wanted to communicate this inner life not only in images, but also in the form of the architecture. This is why the three façades (that of the Nativity, that of the Passion and that of the Glory) are different, because they express different stages in the life of Christ. The naves in the basilica welcome everybody who enters and invite them to gaze upwards and open their hearts. The tree-like columns swoop up to bear the weight of the roofs and the future spires, and at the same time allow the light to flood in through the skylights in the vaults and the stained glass of the windows. From the main entrance the height of the vaulted ceiling rises gradually up to 75 metres by the apse, in the light, slender shapes determined by the architect in a five metre-high model, repeated harmoniously throughout the interior as if in a forest. All this stunning interior forms part of the architectural design shown in the five metre-high model of the main nave built by Gaudí's successors and used for the whole church, according to his plans. Through geometry, and on the basis of his observation of the laws of nature, Gaudí created a design that expressed this nature - considering himself a servant of its Creator - and we,

the architects and builders who have followed Gaudí, can consider ourselves his followers, as we receive his ideas and intentions from the study of his models, mock-ups, plans and writings, and then apply and develop them to make his design a reality.

The arch at the top of the Passion façade and the slender dome of the first sacristy, both recently constructed, are as Gaudí designed them in the last fourteen years of his life, when he devoted himself solely to this church. Like the naves inside, they are designs created with geometrical forms never before used in architecture to produce naturalistic shapes of enormous beauty.

The Sagrada Família has continued to grow since Gaudí's death, over the different generations, each of which has contributed its interest and efforts to make Gaudí's design a reality, together with the artists who have enriched it with their creativity. The book you have before you is testimony to this.

The SAGRADA FAMÍLIA
THE MASTERPIECE OF ART NOUVEAU ARCHITECTURE
Daniel Venteo, historian and museum expert

n 1883, at the age of just 31 and only five years after graduating from the Barcelona School of Architecture, the young Antoni Gaudí i Cornet (1852-1926) was commissioned to direct building work on the new expiatory church of the Holy Family. This commission was to determine the course of his life and his career. While Gaudí began by continuing the work in accordance with the Neo-Gothic design he had inherited from the diocesan architect Francesc de Paula del Villar, from 1892 onwards he poured all his creativity into it and completely transformed the design of the church to give it the appearance it has today. The architect continued to work on the church for the rest of his life, for 43 years until his tragic accidental death in 1926.

There can be no doubt that the Sagrada Família was Antoni Gaudí's most ambitious project and one of the masterpieces of Art Nouveau architecture. His connection with the work on the Sagrada Família was made possible by the architect Joan

Martorell i Montells (1833-1906). The latter was the expert advising the developer behind the new expiatory church: the devout Josep Maria Bocabella (1815-1892), a modest bookseller on the Carrer de la Princesa, in the historic city centre, who had founded the Association of Devotees of Saint Joseph in 1866. This association used its newsletter, *El Propagador de la Devoción a San José*, to publicise its aim of building a new church in the capital city of Catalonia. At that time Barcelona had begun its planned expansion into the new residential neighbourhoods of the Eixample, and Bocabella felt the need to work for the construction of this new cathedral for the new city. It should be emphasised that it was to be an expiatory church, which means it was to be built by public subscription to redeem the individual and collective sins of contemporary society. It is also worth recalling that, at the same time as Bocabella was promoting his popular expiatory church, the influential banker and mayor of the city, Manuel Girona i Agrafel (1818-1905), was using his personal fortune to finance the new façade of Barcelona's Gothic cathedral, unfinished since the 15th century.

THE HOLY FAMILY GROUP

Sculpture of Joseph, Mary and Jesus – the Holy Family that gives its name to the church – over the Charity doorway in the Nativity façade, built in 1958, the work of the sculptor Jaume Busquets.

In 1892, the same year as Bocabella's death, the church project received an enormous anonymous legacy. These resources enabled Gaudí to reinvent the parts of the design that could still be altered once the crypt and part of the apse had been built. The Sagrada Família is a church that fits perfectly into the street plan of the Eixample as designed by Cerdà, even though Gaudí complained about the rigidity of the plan he inherited from the project's original architect. "Upon taking over construction of the Expiatory Church of the Sacred Family, I immediately lamented that the work I found done did not take the diagonal axis of the block and so I prolonged the naves, taking the stairway out of the block and over the Carrer de Mallorca. I did not stop until I reached the final design of the Expiatory Church, of endless possibilities: when I realised there was extra money, when the basilica of Montmartre was completed in Paris I exclaimed, "That will never happen to me!" said Gaudí.

Right from the beginning of construction work, the church became a major attraction, both for the people of

Barcelona and for visitors. As the eminent Australian art critic Robert Hughes stated, "The Sagrada Família remains the symbol of Barcelona, like the Eiffel Tower in Paris or the Harbour Bridge in Sydney." And in fact this is still the case in the 21st century.

"I would not want to finish the work, because it would not be appropriate," declared Gaudí. "A work like this must be the child of a long period, the longer the better. The spirit of the monument must always be preserved, but its life must depend on the generations who pass it on and through which it lives and is formed," proclaimed the brilliant architect. And so it has been. After his death his associate Domènec Sugranyes took over the work. It was continued after the Spanish Civil War by the architects Francesc de Paula Quintana, Isidre Puig i Boada, Lluís Bonet i Garí, Francesc de Paula Cardoner, Jordi Bonet i Armengol and, since 2012, Jordi Faulí. The church is expected to be completed in 2026.

FINAL DESIGN

Overhead view of the interior of the church in all its splendour. Opposite, a model of the final appearance of the Sagrada Família as Antoni Gaudí imagined it before his accidental death in 1926.

AN ICON OF THE BARCELONA SKYLINE

Since construction began in 1882, the Sagrada Família has been an undisputed icon of the Barcelona cityscape. Antoni Gaudí planned for the height of the church not to exceed that of the Montjuïc hill: according to him, a human construction must not over-shadow the work of nature, and therefore of God. "In the Sagrada Família everything is providential: its location in the centre of the city and the plain of Barcelona; it is the same distance from the church to the sea and to the mountains, from Sants and from Sant Andreu, and from the rivers Besòs and Llobre-gat," he declared.

11

FITTING INTO THE CITY

The church occupies one of the blocks in the Eixample district planned by the engineer Ildefons Cerdà in 1859, between the Carrer de Mallorca, Carrer de Provença, Carrer de la Marina and Carrer de Sardenya. Gaudí planned the monumental steps to the Glory façade to extend to the opposite plot, today built on but affected by the city plan.

THE APSE

The apse of the church is topped by the spire of Our Lady, which will be higher than the twelve spires dedicated to the apostles, but not the monumental central spire dedicated to Jesus Christ, topped by a cross. Construction of the first of the two sacristies can be seen on the right of the picture.

THE LANTERN TOWER

172.5 metres high, the central lantern tower of the Sagrada Família, dedicated to Jesus Christ, will be one of the final parts of the structure, together with the Glory façade, completing construction of the church designed by Antoni Gaudí. The spire will be topped by a cross with four arms and a representation of the Lamb of God.

GLORY FAÇADE

Gaudí left only a fragmentary design, barely sketched out, for this façade, which can be seen under construction on the right. "I will neither complete nor develop the model of the spires on the main façade. I have decided simply to leave it sketched out so that another generation can contribute to the church."

THE PASSION FAÇADE

The appearance of the Passion façade contrasts dramatically with the beauty of that of the Nativity: this is just what Gaudí intended. "If I had started by building this façade, people would have complained." In contrast with that of the Nativity, decorated, ornamented, full, that of the Death is hard and bare, as if built of bones. I won't make a model of it, because it is fully prepared with hyperbolic parabolic arches, clearly connected, ready to be made at the time it is built," stated Gaudí. On this page, the steps leading up to the Nativity façade.

THE NATIVITY FAÇADE

The Nativity façade is dedicated to the birth, childhood and adolescence of Jesus. In the words of Antoni Gaudí, "It expresses the hope and joy in life. The spires, topped with the symbols of the apostles and the phrase "Hosanna Excelsis", are devoted to the following apostles, portrayals of which are to be found at the bottom: Barnabas, Simon, Jude and Matthias. Lower down, in ascending rows, the angelic invocations of the Sanctus. The doorways are dedicated to the Christian virtues: the central one to Charity, which is the main one, the one on the right to Faith and the one on the left to Hope," he said.

THE CHARITY DOORWAY

Surmounted by the sculpture of the Holy Family, the Charity doorway is dedicated to the birth of Jesus. In fact, in the words of the architect Jordi Faulí, "The ensemble is a great stone nativity scene." The photographs shows the new doors designed by the sculptor Etsuro Sotoo and the sculpted groups atop the naturalistic pedestals portraying the Three Kings – on the left – and the shepherds – on the right – adoring the divine birth. In the centre of the doorway is the column of Jesus.

THE HOLY FAMILY GROUP

Erected over the Charity doorway on 19th March 1958, Saint Joseph's Day, the sculpted group of the Holy Family was made with stone from Montjuïc and is the work of the artist Jaume Busquets i Mollera (1904-1968).

THE COLUMN OF JESUS

Column supporting the sculpted group of the Holy Family. The ornamental open grille symbolically represents Christ's triumph over sin and was made closely following Antoni Gaudí's instructions. It portrays a palm tree, an allusion to the Tree of Jesse, made up of palm leaves surrounded by a ribbon showing the forty names of Jesus' genealogy according to Matthew 1:2-16.

ETSURO SOTOO

The Japanese sculptor
Etsuro Sotoo (1958) is
the author of the doors in
the Nativity façade. Sotoo
first visited Barcelona
in 1978 and, amazed by
Gaudí's work and the
Sagrada Família, he not
only came to live in the
city but came to work at
the church as a stone-
mason. More than once
Sotoo has declared that
Gaudí is not dead for him,
because he speaks to
him "every day through
the stonework".

INSECTS

Seven metres high and three wide, the doors in the Nativity façade are an invitation to rediscover nature in the tiny details packed with meaning. Each door is unique, recreating ivy, pumpkin and iris leaves and flowers, among which tiny insects and other creatures can be discerned, including ladybirds, snails, spiders, beetles, lizards, butterflies, centipedes, crickets, bees, caterpillars, ants, dragonflies, mites, wasps, flies and locusts.

THE MIRROR OF NATURE

In Etsuro Sotoo's own words, "My goal, and my wish, is to follow Gaudí's line. This means we have to go where Gaudí wanted to go. Placing myself in his shoes. This is when the ideas start to come. Where was Jesus born? Touching the ground, right? So on the door there must be insects, grass. Moreover, the door represents charity. This is why there is ivy, with no flowers."

KINGS AND SHEPHERDS

The existing sculpted groups of the Adoration of the Three Kings and the Shepherds are the work of Joaquim Ros i Bofarull. Originally, Gaudí had envisaged six figures in each group. Before the Spanish Civil War, Joan Matamala (1893-1977) had even produced some preliminary models, of which several historical photographs have survived.

JESUS THE CARPENTER

On the right of the picture, portrayal of the adolescent Jesus as a carpenter. To his right, Joseph and Mary finding him at the temple in Jerusalem. The group was begun by Llorenç Matamala i Piñol (1856-1925) and completed by his son, Joan Matamala.

JAUME BUSQUETS

Sculpted group by Jaume Busquets over the Charity doorway, portraying Jesus, Joseph and Maria, the Holy Family. Its financing was made possible by the contributions of employees at the Barcelona branch of the Banco de Bilbao (Bancobao). These same employees even made a colour film, directed by Vicente Aguado and Fernando Ozores, showing the whole creative process and the speeches given at the inauguration in 1958. Together with the sculpture, a cylinder was included containing a long scroll with all the names of the employees who contributed.

33

ANGELS SINGING

During the Spanish Civil War the original models of the angels singing made by Llorenç Matamala were destroyed. The existing sculptures, which can be seen on the opposite page, are by Etsuro Sotoo. "Creation continues and the Creator is aided by his creatures; those who seek the laws of nature in order to make new pieces are working for the Creator," said Gaudí. On this page, detail of the star of Bethlehem, symbolising the birth of the Messiah.

THE ANNUNCIATION

Scene of the Annunciation by the Archangel Gabriel to Mary, the work of Jaume Busquets, surrounded by a portrayal of the constellations of stars visible in the sky on Christmas Day: from left to right, the signs of Virgo, Leo, Cancer, Gemini, Taurus and Aries.

THE SIGNS
OF THE ZODIAC

On this page, Virgo. To the side, from left to right, portrayal of the constellations of Taurus, Gemini, Cancer and Leo. "Everybody can find something of theirs in the church: farmers see the chickens, scientists the signs of the zodiac, theologians the genealogy of Jesus," declared Gaudí.

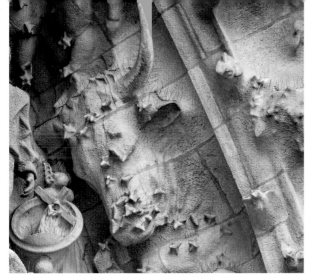

THE TREE OF LIFE

Since its completion in
October 1932, the cypress
tree has been an important
part of the Nativity façade.
For Gaudí it symbolised
eternity and God's love for
men, which the architect
symbolises with white doves.
At the top is Tau, a symbol
of Christ, with the lace of
the love of the Father and
the dove of the Holy Spirit
at the top. On the opposite
page, details of the doves
on the cypress tree and the
angels surrounding - with
incense - the monogram
representing Jesus: JHS,
"Jesus Hominum Salvator",
i.e. "Jesus, saviour of man".
The monogram is beneath a
Greek cross, with the alpha
and omega at the sides.

THE APOSTLES

Figures of four apostles
under the spires on the
Nativity façade, in the tran-
sitional space between their
square base and the circular
shape of the top. They are,
from left to right, Barnabas,
Simon, Jude and Matthias.
All the sculptures were
created by Joan Matamala.
He worked on the church
from 1907, when he was
only fifteen years old, as an
assistant to his father, the
sculptor Llorenç Matamala.

THE ROSARY DOORWAY

The doorway dedicated to Our Lady of the Rosary (Mare de Déu del Roser), connecting the interior of the church to the cloister, was designed by Gaudí himself. It was burnt and largely destroyed by revolutionaries at the beginning of the Spanish Civil War. One of the most valuable pieces of heritage to be damaged was the font, though old photographs of it do survive.

SKYLIGHT

Around this doorway roses are prominently carved in the stone. It was completed by the sculptor Llorenç Matamala in 1899. In the centre the Virgin and Child are portrayed, flanked by Saint Dominic on the left and Saint Catherine on the right. The conical skylight allows a distinctive natural light in at the doorway.

A SYMPHONY OF COLOUR

Entering the church of the Sagrada Família is an explosion of light and colour that is hard to imagine from the outside. Since 1999, the person in charge of making the stained glass windows has been Joan Vila-Grau (1932). "Gaudí wanted the Sagrada Família to be a symphony of colour and light. This is the main instruction he gave us," in the words of the master stained glass maker. "Instead of a set of icons, I opted for a set of colours," he declares.

SYMBOLS

Gaudí precisely specified the set of symbols to be used inside the naves. "The inside of the church will be like a forest. The resemblance comes from the structure of the naves, without having set out to create it deliberately. The columns are helicoidal, because this is the natural shape for a support that bears a load from above, and sloping because the load also has a certain slope resulting from the funicular forms in the vaulting and roof. The supports separate out at the height of the side naves into four others, like the branches of a tree, plus one more which rises up to the vaulting; in their slope, the pillars of the triforium also resemble other smaller branches of colossal trees. The vaulting is decorated with leaves, among which the birds of Catalonia can be seen. The pillars of the central nave are like palms; they are the trees of glory, of sacrifice and of martyrdom. Those in the side naves resemble laurels, trees of glory, of intelligence," explained the architect.

PRESBYTERY

The presbytery was designed by Jordi Bonet i Armengol (1925), chief architect on the Sagrada Família site from 1985 to 2012. The altar is made of a single block of porphyry, originally from Iran. In the background, the organ.

BALDACHIN

The heptagonal baldachin, the canopy over the altar designed by the architect Bonet and inspired by Gaudí's baldachin in Palma cathedral, Mallorca, shows the seven virtues of the Holy Spirit: wisdom, understanding, counsel, fortitude, knowledge, piety, and fear of the Lord, interlaced with the words of the Gloria. The crucifix was made from terracotta by the sculptor Francesc Fajula i Pellicer (1945).

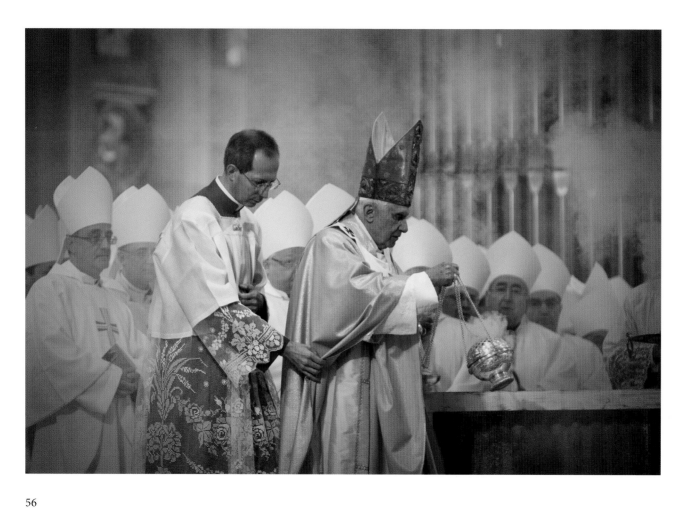

CONSECRATION

The Sagrada Família was consecrated on 7th November 2010 by Pope Benedict XVI, who gave it the title of basilica. Joseph Ratzinger's visit to Barcelona coincided with the anniversary of Pope John Paul II's visit to the Catalan capital 28 years before, in 1982. The church was filled with worshippers and representatives of the authorities. It is estimated that the ceremony was followed by over 1.6 million television viewers in Catalonia.

TETRAMORPH

Where the four central columns come together there is an illuminated tetramorph of the four evangelists: the lion of Mark, the bull of Luke, the angel of Matthew and the eagle of John, designed by the artist from Girona Domènec Fita i Molat (1927).

SAINT GEORGE

Stained glass windows in the eastern façade photographed from the figure of Saint George (Sant Jordi in Catalan) situated on the top of the rood screen. This three metre-high bronze sculpture is by the artist Josep Maria Subirachs i Sitjar (1927-2014). It was installed on 22nd April 2007 - the eve of Saint George's Day - coinciding with the 550th anniversary of the naming of the saint as patron of Catalonia, and the 125th anniversary of the beginning of work on the church of the Sagrada Família.

JOY OF THE SPIRIT

"Glory is light, light gives joy and joy is the happiness of the spirit," were the words of Antoni Gaudí. "In the morning the light comes in through the Nativity façade, where the gentlest, most delicate colours predominate, the greens and blues that are best favoured by the rising sun; in the afternoon the warm tones of the stained-glass windows in the western wall gain in strength with their favourite light, that of the setting sun. And there is a third experience that is totally unexpected, that of artificial light at night. Logically, the colours change but they work perfectly," the master stained glass maker Joan Vila-Grau has explained.

STAINED GLASS WINDOWS

While the upper stained glass windows in the side naves are dedicated to Jesus' parables, the lower stained glass windows in the side naves, transept and central nave feature the names of saints and sanctuaries of the churches portrayed in the columns situated in front of them. On the opposite page, stained glass windows representing the monasteries of Cuixà and the Canigó, and saints Genesius and Ferreolus.

THE STAINED GLASS WINDOWS IN THE APSE

The stained glass windows in the apse are the work of Joan Vila-Grau who, like Gaudí in the last decades of his life, has dedicated himself solely to working on the Sagrada Família. The intention of the master stained glass maker has been, in his own words, to create "an atmosphere that facilitates the vision of the Sagrada Família".

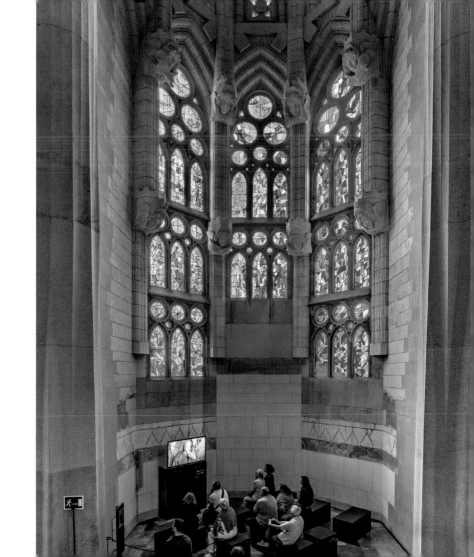

THE SPIRES

The two central spires of the façades of the Nativity and the Passion soar up to 107 metres in height, while the outer two only reach up 98 metres. Gaudí had envisaged installing eighty tubular bells of different lengths and sounds in the spires, turning them into a great organ or carillon which, as the architect Faulí has explained, "would be heard both inside and outside the church".

THE SPIRAL STAIRCASES

Gaudí designed spiral staircases over forty metres long inside the spires of the apostles, both beside the apse and on the Glory façade. All of them were to be complemented, as the architect himself proposed, by strategically-located lifts to allow direct access to the Cross of the Holy Family, the highest point of the whole church, at 172.5 metres above ground level.

THE ROOD SCREEN

Inside the façade of Glory is the rood screen, the inner balcony of the main façade, surmounted by the sculpture of Saint George by Subirachs. Under it is the Lord's Prayer doorway, also by Subirachs. The stained glass windows in the Glory façade in the central nave are in very soft tones in order to let in plenty of natural light to illuminate the ceramic vaults.

CREATIVITY

"The current scarcity of money is what allows me to study the solution to the problems that arise more carefully. Otherwise I would have had to deal with the job of organisation and the technical side of the church would not be so carefully thought-out: they would be more industrial, in that a lot of solutions would have to be repeated. Moreover, in poverty it turns out more elegant, because elegance never appears either rich or opulent. In abundance and complication there is neither elegance nor beauty: there is darkness," argued Gaudí, who invented all kinds of architectural solutions using modest materials in the church.

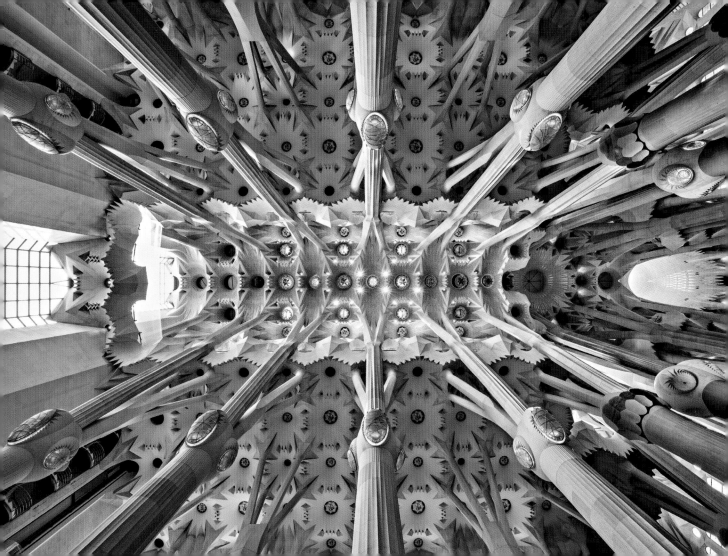

THE FOREST

"The branching form of the columns and their large numbers will give those present the impression of being in a forest," dreamed Gaudí. "This is why at the base of the walls there will be flowing currents of water with gaping fish facing the altar and others going the other way bearing sacramental bread in their mouths."

THE CROSSING

For Gaudí, the lantern tower was, in his own words, "the exaltation of the church: it has an outer and an inner life, it must light the altar, as the crossing is the darkest place in the church; over it should be the topmost part of the building to accentuate the pyramidal shape" the architect wanted to give the church. This is the setting the visitor to the church finds at the crossing. "The four columns supporting the lantern tower will be of iron, because of the great weight they have to bear. If they were of stone they would take up more space, right in the centre of the church," he explained. On the opposite page, the columns and the central vault of the apse.

THE TRINITARIAN TRIANGLE

A representation of the Eternal Father with the trinitarian triangle in the principal lantern tower in the apse. "It is not to be regretted that I cannot finish the church; I will grow old," stated Gaudí, "And others will have to come along in my place; like that it will be even more wonderful." If Tarragona Cathedral, for example, had been completed by the same person as began it, it would not be so rich. In time other talented artists made their mark on it, and everything in there is beautiful." This was Gaudí's idea, made real in the building of the Sagrada Família.

THE COLUMNS

All the columns in the church have a structural reason and a symbolic meaning determined by Gaudí himself: the four columns at the crossing bear the names of the evangelists and support the tower of Jesus Christ, while the rest are named after the apostles and the apostolic churches founded by them. The columns in the transept naves bear the name of Catalan dioceses, and the rest of the columns in the central and side naves are dedicated to the rest of the dioceses in the former Crown of Aragon, the other Spanish archdioceses and also those of Europe, the Americas, Africa and Asia.

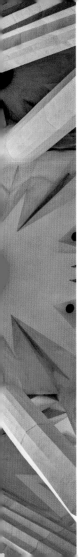

THE CENTRAL NAVE

The structural architectural "trees" in the central nave, built of granite, divide into two branches. The first and highest rises to 45 metres in height, supporting the vaulting and roof over the central nave, as shown on the opposite page. The second of the branches ends at a height of thirty metres to support the vaulting of the side naves and the large window openings in the central nave. In the words of the architect Faulí, "Gaudí invented a column that was a first in the history of architecture."

THE SIDE NAVES

Built from white cement, the columns in the side naves subtly vary in their shapes in ways that pass practically unnoticed by the visitor. The base of the branches is either square or pentagonal in shape, though they change rapidly in the first few metres to end up practically round. In Gaudí's opinion, in executing surfaces geometry did not complicate construction, but simplified it.

A CHURCH FOR THE WORLD

"We must all contribute to the building of the Sagrada Família, as it must be the church of a whole people," stated Antoni Gaudí at the beginning of the 20th century. "Barcelona's rapid growth in fifty years, having quadrupled its population, has crystallised in the Sagrada Família: a church, the only thing worthy to represent a people, as religion is the highest aspect of man." In the 21st century, the visitors and worshippers who visit the Sagrada Família every day now come from all over the planet.

THE COLOUR OF THE SUN

The architect and essayist Joan Bergós i Massó (1894-1974) recalled that Gaudí had exclaimed more than once that, "The sun is the greatest painter of the Mediterranean lands." And he made this a reality in his design for the Sagrada Família, in a constant dialogue between horizontality and verticality that certainly had profound spiritual implications: in the church, according to Gaudí, the decoration was based "on the saints ascending from earth to heaven and the angels descending from heaven to the earth".

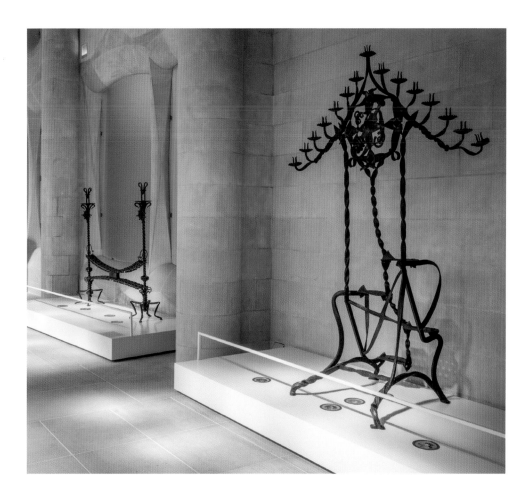

THE WESTERN SACRISTY

The new western sacristy, opened in early 2016, features some of the most valuable historical items preserved from the time of Antoni Gaudí himself. This is the case of the two cupboards in the sacristy: one is used to store the liturgical items worn by celebrants and priests in services, and the other for the different liturgical objects, such as chalices and patens.

A NEW ARCHITECTURAL MILESTONE

Completion of the new sacristy was a further milestone in the history of the construction of the church, which is expected to be finished by 2026. With a basement level and five storeys topped by a dome with windows, this is the first of the two sacristies planned by Gaudí, which will be connected to each other and to the inside of the church through the perimeter cloister once construction is complete.

ORIGINAL AND RESTORED HERITAGE

The original objects exhibited in the cloister of the new sacristy include the cast iron candelabra designed by Gaudí himself around 1898 for the church crypt, as well as the cross candelabra and the tabletop candlesticks he designed around 1890, also for services in the crypt. Another of the objects on show is a reconstruction of the portable throne designed by the architect for preaching, which was destroyed during the civil war.

THE CRYPT

Overview of the crypt. Built between 1882 and 1889, it is ten metres below the apse. Around the central vaulting is the ambulatory and seven chapels dedicated to the Holy Family: Saint Joseph in the centre; to his left the Sacred Heart, Saint Anne and Saint John; and to his right the Immaculate Conception, Saint Joaquim and finally the chapel dedicated to Saint Elisabeth and Saint Zacharias.

THE CENTRAL VAULT

View of the central vault of the crypt and the three altars: the sacristy, the central altar and the altar of Our Lady of Montserrat. "In Barcelona Cathedral they put the steps down into the crypt in the central nave. This solution became fashionable and was adopted in other Gothic churches. But it is a mistake and the proof is that, when an important celebration comes along, they first thing they have to do is cover the steps with a platform. This is why in the Sagrada Família, instead of stairs down to the crypt in the centre, we put two at the sides, at the angles between the crossing and the apse," argued Gaudí.

THE ANNUNCIATION

The keystone to the central vault in the crypt, in fine polychrome, represents the scene of the Annunciation by the Archangel Gabriel to the Virgin Mary, the work of the sculptor from Manresa Joan Flotats i Llucià (1847-1917). His son-in-law and disciple was the sculptor Llorenç Matamala.

THE CHAPEL OF SAINT JOSEPH

On the walls of the chapel of Saint Joseph are carved the arms of the Dalmases-Clarasó family, linked to the developer of the church, Josep Maria Bocabella, and the Castellbell family, who sponsored construction of the altar. The wood carving of Saint Joseph is the work of Maximí Sala Sánchez, who died in 1895. On the opposite page, detail of the relief of the Holy Family by Josep Llimona i Bruguera (1864-1934), in a frame designed by Gaudí himself, the work of the Genoese artist Mario Maragliano Navone (1864-1944).

ANTONI GAUDÍ'S TOMB

Beside the altars in the
crypt is the chapel of Our
Lady of Mount Carmel,
with Antoni Gaudí's tomb,
which was seriously
damaged by revolution-
aries during the Spanish
Civil War. The figure of
Our Lady is the work
of Jaume Busquets.
In the chapel of Christ
Crucified is the tomb of
Josep Maria Bocabella.

LAMPS

The seven chapels in the crypt are dedicated to the family of Jesus; in the centre is Saint Joseph. This was the first part of the church to be completed and opened for worship, in the year 1885. On these pages, details of the artistic lamps that serve to light the chapel of Our Lady of Mount Carmel.

THE PAIN OF LIFE

In Gaudí's words, the Passion façade "expresses the truth and pain of life". The spires bear the same symbols and inscriptions as on the Nativity façade. They are dedicated to and bear the images of the apostles Saint James the Less, Saint Bartholomew, Saint Thomas and Saint Phillip. There are three doorways, dedicated to the Christian virtues: Faith, Hope and Charity. They are in a porch with five arches covered across its full width by a gallery representing Limbo."

THE DOORS
OF THE PASSION

The Passion façade has four bronze doors, made by the sculptor Josep Maria Subirachs, which include the text of the Passion according to the Gospel of Matthew and John in the design of the two centre doors, turned into the pages of a kind of monumental sculpted book.

JOSEP MARIA SUBIRACHS

The doors in the Passion façade are filled with iconographic references, often closely linked to the creative imagination of the artist Subirachs. In these images a fragment of the Scriptures can be seen, accompanied by various details included in the text in a highly subtle way by the sculptor.

117

THE SIDE DOORS

The side doors in the Passion façade, designed by Subirachs, recreate the prayer in the Garden of Gethsemane while the apostles sleep, as shown on this page, the scene with the crown of thorns and Jesus before Herod and Pilate - the latter on the opposite page.

SCULPTURE

In 1986, the Building Committee of the church commissioned the sculpture on the Passion façade to Josep Maria Subirachs. In the words of Jordi Faulí, the sculpted group created by the artist "is one of the most important produced in the world" in the late 20th century.

THE LAST SUPPER

To the left of the Faith doorway, this portrayal of the Last Supper is the first of the sculpted groups that surmount the Passion façade. The artist has placed a dog at Judas' feet as a symbol of loyalty.

THE EUCHARIST

The figure of Jesus Christ, on the left for visitors entering the church, at the moment when he institutes the Eucharist with his disciples, the apostles. The photograph shows an unusual point of view, with a view of the city in the background.

123

THE APOSTLES

Portraits of apostles sculpted by Josep Maria Subirachs for the sculpted group of the Last Supper. These are among the hundred sculptures created by the artist for the church of the Sagrada Família.

JUDAS' KISS

On the opposite page, detail of Judas' kiss and of the cryptogram in which Subirachs represented the age of Christ using 310 possible arithmetical combinations.

FLAGELLATION

The image of the flagellation of Christ tied to the column symbolises his solitude at the sixth station of the cross. This is alone in the middle of the doors in the Passion façade. Behind, at the threshold, are alpha and omega, the beginning and the end.

THE DENIAL OF PETER

Details of the sculpted group of the fourth station of the cross: the denial of Peter and the figure of the cock. Next to this, on the right, detail of the labyrinth, an allegory of the spiritual path of believers which is present in mediaeval cathedrals like Chartres, admired by Antoni Gaudí.

ECCE HOMO

According to John 19:5, Ecce homo – "Behold the man" – were the words of the Roman governor Pontius Pilate when the scourged Jesus was presented to him. Beside this, Pilate washing his hands, accompanied by his wife Claudia Procula, mentioned in the Gospel of Matthew.

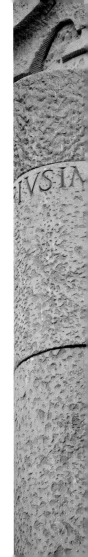

JESUS CARRIES THE CROSS

Jesus Christ carries the cross, speaks and consoles the women of Jerusalem, at the ninth station of the cross. In the centre of the scene, Veronica holds the cloth with the face of Christ. Subirachs included two specific references to Gaudí in this group: he used his appearance for the person witnessing the scene and recreated the chimney tops of La Pedrera in the helmets of the Roman soldiers.

THE SOLDIER LONGINUS

"One of the soldiers pierced his side with a spear, and immediately blood and water came out," according to John 19:34. This scene was portrayed by Subirachs with the peculiarity that the soldier thrusts the spear into the Passion façade itself, which represents Christ.

SOLDIERS AND DICE

Portrayal of the soldiers who have crucified Christ as they play dice for his clothes. "They gambled for his clothes by throwing dice," according to Matthew 27:35.

135

THE CRUCIFIXION OF CHRIST

Christ crucified, with Our Lady, Saint John and Mary Magdalene on his right. At the foot of the cross is a skull, the symbol of Adam. This is the thirteenth and penultimate station of the cross.

DESCENT AND ENTOMBMENT

The fourteenth and final station of the cross is the descent and entombment of Christ, shown here with the figures of Joseph of Arimathea, holding his head, and Nicodemus, holding his feet. Subirachs used his own self-portrait for the appearance of the latter character. Our Lady is also shown, with an Easter egg, symbolising the Resurrection.

CITY VIEWS

Ever since the church first began to take on its characteristic verticality, the spires have been excellent viewpoints overlooking the Barcelona cityscape. In the background, the profile of the Collserola ridge with the city at its feet.

MEN'S GOOD WORKS

The tops of the windows in the side naves are crowned with naturalistic mosaic portrayals of chestnuts, persimmons, figs and almonds, the work of the Japanese sculptor Etsuro Sotoo. They represent the good work of men inspired by the Holy Spirit.

CHALICE AND HOST

Pinnacles of the central nave with the portrayal by Etsuro Sotoo of the eucharistic symbols of the chalice and the grape, and the host and the corn, respectively. These pieces are directly inspired by the models left by Antoni Gaudí.

THE CHURCH AND BARCELONA

The Sagrada Família is a church that fits perfectly into the street plan of the Eixample as designed by Cerdà, even though Gaudí complained about the rigidity of the plan he inherited from the project's original architect.

THE GARGOYLES ON THE APSE

The gargoyles on the apse represent the wildlife that was typical of the spot when construction of the church began in the 1880s, including snails, different types of lizard, frogs, toads, salamanders and snakes, acting as drains for rainwater since the 1890s. These gargoyles were Llorenç Matamala's first work on the church.

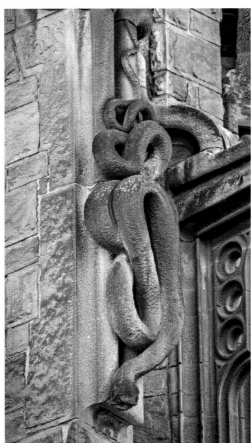

147

THE NATURAL SETTING

Carvings of ears of plants that were common around the church over a century ago, immortalised by Gaudí at the pinnacles of the buttresses of the apse in the 1890s. The apse has eight buttresses, dedicated to the founders of historic religious orders: Clare, Bruno, Bernard, Benedict, Scholastica and Anthony the Abbott, together with Francis of Assisi and Teresa of Jesus.

INSPIRING FEAR

"Some may find this façade extravagant, but I would even like it to be frightening, and to do this I will not stint on the light and dark, relief features and hollows, even if the result gives the most dismal impression. What is more, I am prepared to sacrifice the construction itself, to break up arches, to cut up columns, to give an idea of how bitter the sacrifice is," declared Antoni Gaudí about the Passion façade.

POPULAR CULTURE

Gaudí explained how, on one occasion, "A person who was unenthusiastic about the church of the Sagrada Família, when he heard that the stained glass in the windows would have figures of saints one above the other, said scornfully that they would look like the Xiquets de Valls [a group famous for constructing the traditional Catalan human towers]. I replied that if that were the case it would not be a defect, but would reinforce the symbolism, as nobody can get to heaven by his own means, but to get there we must depend on each other," argued the architect who, like the Xiquets de Valls, was from the southern province of Tarragona.

GLASS MOSAIC

"If I had used ceramic tiles instead of glass mosaic, this spire would not have the quality it has, because the enamels would be cast at low temperatures and over the base material," explained the architect Antoni Gaudí.

154

EPISCOPAL ATTRIBUTES

The spires are topped by pinnacles representing the episcopal attributes: the crozier, the ring, the mitre and the cross, with the inscription "Hosanna Excelsis" under each of them. "Look at this top...! Doesn't it seem to join heaven and earth? These brightly-coloured mosaics are the first thing sailors will see as they approach Barcelona: it will be a radiant welcome!" exclaimed Gaudí.

GOLD MOSAICS

In Gaudí's own words, "Those that cover the top of the spire are made of the ordinary glass used in green bottles, which is stronger than the other kind. The golden tone comes from melting the glass and, while it is still viscous and spread out to form a layer, adding gold leaf; as gold melts at a lower temperature, it fuses with the surface of the glass to make a single mass," explained the architect.

THE CHURCH SQUARES

The current Plaça de la Sagrada Família and Plaça d'Antoni Gaudí were laid out in the years 1928 and 1981 respectively. The first was officially given the name of General Barrera in November 1927, and designed by Nicolau Maria Rubió i Tudurí (1891-1981), who had to wait almost half a century to see work begin on the second. The architect died four months before he could see the work completed.

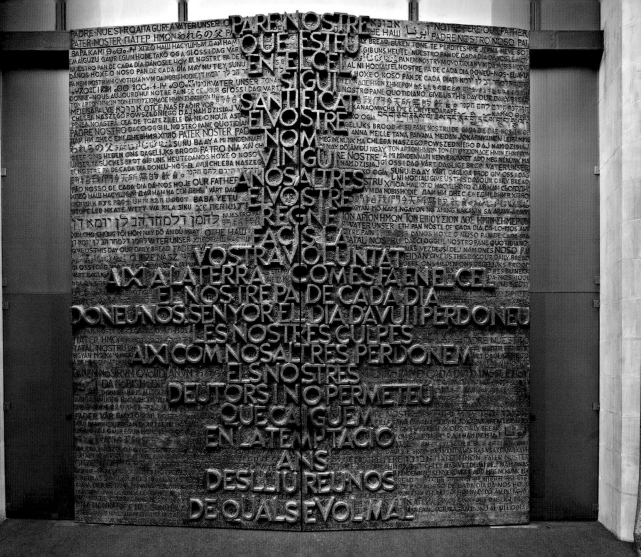

THE LORD'S PRAYER

This monumental Lord's Prayer in bas-relief occupies the centre doors of the Glory façade, leading into the central nave. As well as Catalan, the words can also be found in fifty other languages. The door handles are a homage to Antoni Gaudí, taking his initials, A and G.

164

THE GLORY DOORS

The monumental doors in the Glory façade were also made by the sculptor Josep Maria Subirachs, with the assistance of the sculptor from Tarragona Bruno Gallart Pardo (1941). There are seven doors, each of which is dedicated to a sacrament: baptism, confirmation, eucharist, penitence, ordination, marriage and unction of the sick.

THE CLOISTER

Gaudí envisaged side cloisters that would connect together the whole church of the Sagrada Família without needing to go inside it. The sections already built house various exhibition spaces, like that devoted to Gaudí and nature, which can be seen on the opposite page.

MODEL OF
THE GÜELL CRYPT

The Sagrada Família's historic collection also includes a reconstruction from 1982 of the spectacular large-scale polyfunicular model created by Gaudí to study the design of the industrial settlement of Santa Coloma de Cervelló, in the Baix Llobregat.

MODEL OF THE INTERIOR

1:10 scale model of the central nave of the church exhibited in the Sagrada Família's historic collection. The original was destroyed during the Spanish Civil War. Visitors can literally walk through the scale inside of the church, just as Gaudí himself and his workers did.

THE MODEL-MAKERS' WORKSHOP

The work of the model-makers' workshop carries on in the 21st century, with plaster models and others made using a 3D printer, alongside the work done by the architects, who today exploit computer systems for structural analysis, drawing and calculation which are very useful.

RECONSTRUCTION

Most of the working models and the historic documentation left by Gaudí after his death in 1926 were violently destroyed ten years later, on the outbreak of the civil war. From 1939 onwards, the Building Committee began to reconstruct them, often with the aid of historic photographs like these shots of the model-makers' workshop.

THE SCHOOL

In late 1908 Gaudí designed a small temporary school for the workers' children and needy children from the neighbourhood, at one of the corners of the church construction site. Together with Gaudí's workshop, the building was burnt down by revolutionaries in July 1936. After the war it was rebuilt and finally, in 2002, it was moved to its current site, a few metres away from the original location, to allow work to continue on the cloisters and the Glory façade.

THE SACRED HEART CLASSROOM

Like the rest of the school, the interior of the Sacred Heart classroom was photographed in detail by Adolf Mas, which later allowed it to be reconstructed in detail.

LE CORBUSIER

On the opposite page, a view of the undulating roof and walls of the church school with their conical shapes. On a visit to the Sagrada Família in 1928, the prestigious architect Le Corbusier was amazed at the simplicity and solidity of the system of construction envisaged by Gaudí.

THE EXPIATORY CHURCH

"The church of the Sagrada Família is made by the people and mirrors them," stated Gaudí. The architect himself realised over a hundred years ago that it should be assumed that, "Work on this church will be long-term, something that is true of all churches of outstanding grandeur, which took centuries to build." With their contributions visitors make it possible to continue the work. In 2012 the Sagrada Família had over 3.2 million visitors from all five continents.

AVINGUDA DE GAUDÍ

In 1908 and 1916, Gaudí was consulted by the city council about the town planning around the church. The architect proposed creating open spaces in the form of a star-shaped square that would, as he put it, create "the minimum distances and viewpoints required for normal views of the church." However, the council did not take up the architect's proposals and the surrounding plots continued to be classed as building land. Only in 1926 did the Avinguda de Gaudí begin to be opened, then named after the Spanish dictator of the day, Primo de Rivera.

MASTERPIECES
OF ART NOUVEAU

The expiratory church of the
Sagrada Família, by Antoni
Gaudí, photographed from
the administration building
of the Santa Creu i Sant Pau
hospital, designed by the
architect Lluís Domènech
i Montaner (1850-1923).
Both constructions, listed
as World Heritage Sites by
UNESCO, are masterpieces
of Modernisme, the Catalan
branch of Art Nouveau, and
of world architecture.

Index